BORN TO CATHART!

BORN TO CATHART!

(Laughing Your Way Through Stress)

by Marion E. Pietz

Born to Cathart!

Copyright © 1999
Marion E. Pietz

ALL RIGHTS RESERVED
No portion of this publication may be reproduced, stored in an electronic system, or transmitted in any form or by any means, electronic, mechanical, photocopy, recording or otherwise, without written permission from the author. Brief quotations may be used in literary reviews.

ISBN: 0-7392-0151-4

Printed in the United States of America
By Morris Publishing • 3212 E Hwy 30 • Kearney, NE 68847

Illustrations and cover design by Sharalan Crawford, Houston, Texas, (281) 537-5875.

Born To Charthart

To My Nieces & Nephews:
Peter, Catherine, Gordon, Lisa, John, James & Danny.

Don't ever forget–it is your heritage to laugh!

TABLE OF CONTENTS

Preface 9

Acknowledgments 11

Chapter One – Born to Cathart! 13

Chapter Two – There's A Tape Player in Your Head 21

Chapter Three – Like a Medicine 27

Chapter Four – But? What If I . . .? 39

Chapter Five – Appreciators and Presenters 47

Chapter Six – Ten Irrational Beliefs About Laughter 53

Chapter Seven – Laughter and Other Emotions 63

Chapter Eight – Black Crayons 73

Chapter Nine – Pull My Finger! 81

Bibliography 83

PREFACE

My mission in life is to help resurrect laughter in the lives of individuals in a stressful world. As I travel the country giving workshops on *Laughing Your Way Through Stress*, many people have asked me to put my thoughts into a book. I don't profess to say anything new or profound within the pages of this literary attempt. I realize that it may be only a repetition of what you already know about laughter. However, repetition is a good teacher.

My philosophy is simple—"*A merry heart doeth good like a medicine*" (Proverbs 17:22). This truth has been right before our eyes for thousands of years. We all need our daily dose of mirth medicine. After all, if He is our Great Physician, then we need to do what the doctor prescribes.

We live in a world that has many problems which we cannot always escape. I like to think of laughter as an oasis in the desert journey of life. We can drink in the medicinal effects of laughter at each oasis.

Take time to discover the laughter for yourself. Incorporate mirth into your life every day. Take healing intervals of hearty laughter for fifteen seconds each day, and see if you don't realize the rejuvenating and energizing effects of a good laugh.

Life is not a dress rehearsal. We do not get a second chance at this thing called living. This is it! Laughter makes the journey more healthy and enjoyable. Laughter may not change your situation, but it can change *you* in the situation. And that is what is important!

It is my hope that you will be able to open yourself to laughter and to all the other positive emotions (joy, hope, faith, love, encouragement, etc.) that await to enhance your life.

I hope that you enjoy *Born To Cathart!* and that you will always remember that you were born to be a CATHARTER! Remember: This laugh is on me. Pull My Finger!

Born To Cathart

Born To Cathart

Acknowledgments

It is a wonderful heritage to have a laughing family. My everlasting thanks to my parents, Peter J. and Julianna M. Pietz, for having me and for allowing me to grow up laughing.

To Carole and Helmut, thanks for being my sounding board and audience.

To Peter and Katie, I love the *"catharter"* in both of you.

To Jack and Elsie, *Sons of the Desert*, here is another fine mess you've gotten me into!

Special thanks to my Uncles Eddie and Jerry, the "Kings" of the great laughs and one liners. You help set the example for us all.

To my Aunts Elizabeth and Kay, two great appreciators of laughter. You are never to be forgotten. Your humorous stories and the music live on.

Thanks to Uncles Gordon and Johnny for being men of character and easy laughers. You make coming home a joy. I love you both. You have taught me many valuable lessons in life, especially to love, sing, and laugh.

No book is written just by the author. A very special thanks to Mary L. Schano, who volunteered to type the manuscript of this book from some very bad tape recordings. It was love above and beyond the call of duty. Thanks Mary L.; God will reward you abundantly. And if I sell this book, I may send you a few bucks as well. I love and appreciate you.

Thanks to Kay, my business coach and friend. Thank you for all the suggestions, encouragement, belief, listening and laughing at my foibles. You are an appreciator of humor. Dreams do come true. Thanks for helping this one come to pass.

To Steve and Nelda, for keeping my computer up and running.

To the edit party crew . . . I couldn't have done it without you.

Born To Cathart

To all my laughing friends and church family . . . I couldn't laugh without you.

To my "Laughing Pastor" and his wife, thank you for teaching me to take living for God seriously and myself lightly.

Last, but always first in my life, Jesus Christ. I thank God for His many blessings and gifts, especially the gift of laughter.

Born To Cathart

God laughs because He knows more than we do.
God has sharper vision.
  Miriam Pollard

Chapter One

Born to Cathart!

After three years of Latin in a Catholic High School, you would think I'd remember more than, **"AMO, AMAS, AMAT!"** I know that has something to do with love, but don't ask this old maid what it is! It's not that I didn't try to get married; in fact, I tried real hard. One time I took out an ad in a newspaper advertising for a husband, and I got lots of replies. They all said, *"You can have mine!"* Of course, I'm at that difficult age for a woman when I'm too young for Medicare but too old for men to care. I tried all sorts of methods to find a good man. Even that stud finder I bought at the hardware store didn't work.

Therefore, the only thing I ever got to do with that verb was conjugate it. I repeated that conjugation so many times that I knew the old saying rang true:

"Latin is dead, as dead as it could be.
It first killed the Romans,
And now it's killing me!"

A Rhodes scholar I was not. Maybe that's why my interests turned to mischief.

In Junior Biology class, I found a box of dry kidney beans. Don't ask me why, but I stuffed my blazer pockets full of them. And with a spiritual, reverent look on my face, I walked into my next class–Religion. Like all mischievous students, I took my seat in the back of the classroom. My teacher was Sister Alice Marie. Naturally, with a name like

Born To Cathart

that, my friends and I nicknamed her–*Sammy*!

Each time *Sammy* turned around to write something on the blackboard, I threw a few of those kidney beans around the room. The "rat-tat-tat" sound they made reminded me of a machine gun blast. *Sammy* turned around so fast it surprised me. For an old nun, she could really move! She cast her eyes to the back of the room right toward "Little Miss Innocence" who pretended to be waiting for the next religious revelation.

I'll never forget the Christmas of 1963. Dear old *Sammy* spent hours decorating her bulletin boards to reflect the Christmas season. A picture of the Holy Family, colored all with crayons, adorned the back wall. There in full color was Blessed Mother in blue, Saint Joseph in brown, baby Jesus with a bright yellow halo around his head and a big pile of fluffy yellow hay underneath the manger.

Every day, my friends and I would find more sadistic ways to drive *Sammy* nuts. One girl fell out of the clothes closet pretending to have a fit. Another day, we became a herd of animals from Old McDonald's farm singing in her classroom. It became a challenge to create novel ways to disturb *Sammy's* class.

A few days after *Sammy* put up her bulletin boards, I started with my fake sneezes. I took my seat in the back of the room right in front of the bulletin board with the manger scene. When the time was just right, I let out a big . . . Aaaaaaaaaah Chooooooooooo!

I continued to sneeze until an exasperated nun turned around and hollered at me, "Marion! What is wrong with your nose?"

"I dink I'm allergic to da hay!" I replied with a stuffed up voice.

"What hay?" she countered.

I pointed to the bulletin board behind me and said, "Da hay in da nativity dene."

Sammy then proceeded to explain that I couldn't be allergic to the hay because it was only a picture colored with crayons.

"Yeah, I know!" I answered. "I dinks it's dycoso-matic!"

At the end of that year, *Sammy* retired.

In high school, I wanted to be a cheerleader. I could see my-

Born To Cathart

self racing onto the basketball court in my little green and gold skirt with my pom-poms in hand. There I would be standing before a wild, enthusiastic crowd, leading them in a victory cheer.

I loved pep rallies. School spirits aflame! In addition, they got me out of classes for the afternoon. The pep rally was the only time in Catholic school that the students could cut up and make some noise. In fact, it was the only time in Catholic high school that you knew girls had hips.

Standing in the bleachers, the girls would swing their hips back and forth to the rhythm of the cheer in honor of the boys on the basketball team. For the sake of school spirit, the good sisters suppressed their temptation to tell us to sit down, be still and be quiet.

You see, nuns found it hard to acknowledge hips, especially swaying hips. Back then, the sisters only acknowledged body parts from the neck up. Everything below the head was a sin or a near occasion of sin! Those nuns were pretty strict. Of course, it's not that the girls wanted to commit any mortal or even venial sins. But start talking about those handsome, sexy basketball players, and soon they'd be entertaining those "near occasions of sin."

Although the nuns were as strict as could be, they didn't hold a candle to a *novena-making Momma*. The fear of God and a novena-making Momma kept many a daughter from committing any mortal, venial or even those near occasions of sins. For those of you who may not know, a novena is bombarding heaven with your prayers about a certain issue. Every Monday night, you would find hundreds of Catholic mothers gathered at St. Gregory's, singing and praying in unison. Seeing all those women praying was a combination hard to beat.

When my sister and I contemplated doing anything against Mom's desires, all she had to announce was, "Alright! Go ahead! But I'm going to make a novena." God, Mom and novenas were just too much for any child to overcome.

Cheerleaders were always the cute, little petite girls with blonde hair and big dimples and were usually well endowed. I

Born To Cathart

happened to be the tallest, skinniest and most unendowed girl in the school. So they made me part of the rosary team. I got to be one of those *little* beads.

Fortunately, I get to fulfill my cheerleading fantasy when doing my *Laughing Your Way Through Stress* workshops. I ask the participants to pretend they are high school students at a pep rally, and I lead them in the following cheer:

   I...
      WAS...
         BORN...
            TO...
               CATHART!

That's right! I said... *Cathart!*

The word *cathart* is a derivative of the word *catharsis*, which we associate with the medical community. Catharsis means to release, purge and let go. Now you should understand why we associate it with the medical community. When someone is in the hospital, he or she is usually *catharting* from one end or the other.

An elderly gentleman, sitting in the back at one of my workshops, apparently couldn't hear too well. When he heard that he was born to *cathart*, he must have thought I was saying another word that rhymed with *cathart!* He turned to his wife, who couldn't hear any better, and asked, "What does she want us to do?"

His wife replied, "Don't worry! You do it all the time!"

Why do I tell people that they were born to cathart? When God, the almighty wise creator, formed us out of the dust of the earth, He breathed into us the breath of life, giving us the ability to physically and emotionally release, purge and let go of the things that hurt us. He gave us catharting.

※ ※ ※ ※ ※ ※ ※

As you sit reading this book, do you realize that the rest of the world is outside of the room where you are sitting? Think about it. Almost everything that could possibly disturb, frustrate,

Born To Cathart

and anger you or wreak havoc in your life is outside the room where you are sitting. And do you know what they are doing? They are waiting for you–waiting to annoy, upset and bother you. However, they are not bothering or upsetting you now. Moreover, as soon as you come into contact with all those people, places and things, you are going to do a very powerful thing. You are going to interpret what they mean to you. You are the one to decide if they will become a stressor in your life. This probably makes you want to stay right where you are, doesn't it?

She is out there! The woman who drives me crazy. Like chalk screeching down a blackboard, she sends chills up and down my spine. Dutifully, she stands behind the salad bar at a local cafeteria where I usually eat. She's waiting to greet me with that monotone, flat, unenthusiastic voice of hers. Without fail she asks me, "Do you wan...na sal...aaad?"

I am probably going to die of colon cancer because I am not getting enough roughage, and it is all her fault. Ah, but alas, in reality I know it is not she who stresses me. That woman has no power over me other than what I choose to give her. When I start to think that she is a stressor, then that is what she becomes to me.

Psychological stress is nothing more than a result of the thoughts you think. The trouble starts when you begin acting on those thoughts. Turning fifty is usually a difficult stressor for most people. Fifty is the age where the broadness of your mind and the narrowness of your hips exchange places. My father used to say that life begins at fifty. My mother used to say, "Begins to what?" I find at fifty that the men who used to sit up and notice me are now too old to stand up and follow me.

The reason I did not bungee cord jump today is that I told myself, "Marion, you could die!" But that did not stop many people from tying ropes around their ankles and jumping off towers and cliffs, hoping they stop just before their face smashes into the ground. The only difference between us is the way we think.

Think about a traffic jam. At this moment, highway traffic is not bothering you. You're not experiencing it. However, when you

Born To Cathart

are in the midst of it . . . you'll think about what it means to you.

Where does road rage come from? Surprisingly, it doesn't come from that elderly woman driving aimlessly through town in her beige sedan, barely able to see over the steering wheel. On the contrary, it comes from your own negative or irrational self-talk. You can choose to think thoughts that upset you or thoughts that calm and relax you. The choice is yours. The way you think will determine your feelings and directly affect your behavior.

Remember getting that test booklet in high school or college? Carefully, you would pick out all the easy problems to answer first. About thirty minutes into the test, you would begin to hear an annoying, distracting sound. It was a sniffle.

At first, you would just glance over at the *sniffling* student. Only a few minutes later, there it was again! Perhaps you found yourself even writing the word "sniffle" as one of your test answers. You would ask yourself, "Why doesn't he blow his nose?!" (Did you ever notice that people who have runny noses never seem to have any tissues with them? They just sit there and sniff it up!)

Every time you heard a sniffle, you would turn your head sharply at the offending student, hoping they could read that the daggers in your eyes, the steam coming from your ears, and the drool dripping from your mouth meant for them to stop. You were ready to choke every sniffle out of that student. However, you whispered angrily, "Why don't you blow your nose?!"

They looked at you and responded, "Who, me?"

They continued sniffling, and you failed the test.

When you came into contact with that sniffle, you began to interpret what it meant to you. Your interpretation wasn't the same as the other students in the classroom. Why? They were able to tune the sniffler out of their conscious minds. In fact, they never even noticed the sniffler, and they passed the test. Because they were thinking differently than you, they passed and you failed.

❋ ❋ ❋ ❋ ❋ ❋

Born To Cathart

There are two types of dangers in the world. The first danger is a real danger. There is an actual threat to your life or to someone else you love. When something outside of yourself is a real danger, like someone pointing a gun at your head, your mind sends a signal to your body to react and protect you. The body then goes into the fight or flight response. Fight and flight are gifts from God to keep you safe.

The second type of danger is a perceived danger. These are the dangers where you tell yourself to feel angry, nervous or upset, like when you are sitting in a traffic jam. You're stuck and going nowhere fast. Questions keep running through your mind, "Why is this traffic here? I'm going to be late! Don't they know who I am? Where did all these people come from?"

I'm reminded of the story I heard about a businessman who was experiencing a bad travel day. Apparently, he had been bumped, rerouted, redirected and grounded so many times that he lost his patience with everyone. He marched himself up to the ticket counter, demanding to be seated on the next flight. He hollered, cursed and made a big scene. Trying to keep cool, the attendant simply told the businessman that she was doing everything possible. In a loud, hostile tone, the man slammed his fist on the counter and shouted many times, "Do you know who I am? Do you know who I am?"

With that, the attendant got on the loudspeaker and announced, "Ladies and gentlemen, may I have your attention. There seems to be a man up here who doesn't know who he is. If anybody could come forth and identify him, it would be greatly appreciated." The attendant did not let this man's ranting and raving intimidate her. However, the poor man looked like he was about to have a coronary.

Repeat the following words out loud ... MY BODY IS STUPID! I say that because your body doesn't know the difference between a real and a perceived danger, so it reacts the same to both. When your mind tells your body there's a danger, real or perceived, the fight and flight response kicks in to protect you.

Born To Cathart

The fight and flight response is your inner security guard on duty twenty-four hours a day. When you find yourself walking down a dark street, your security guard commands physiological changes to occur in order to prepare you to flee or fight. A Harvard study indicated that from 60 to 90 percent of doctor visits were due to stress related problems.

Which danger do you think is putting people in the doctor's offices, the real dangers or the perceived ones? I think our security guard is working over-over-time, and it's killing us slowly but surely.

You probably would not see stress listed as the cause of death on a death certificate. However, many physical complaints that are brought to the doctor's office have their origins in stress.

Throughout his many works, Dr. Wayne Dyer, Ph.D., states that whatever you think about will expand. Start thinking that someone is looking in your window or is outside your door. Keep thinking about it, and soon you'll find yourself peeking out the window or checking to see if you locked the front door. It probably won't be the first time you scare yourself. Now think about sucking on a big, juicy yellow lemon. If you're like most people, you had a physical reaction to a thought. Well, that's how psychological stress works.

Human beings are constantly upsetting themselves by their own interpretations of people, places and things outside of themselves. You are making yourself a nervous wreck, a rageoholic, and a depression case because of your thoughts. Are you helpless? No, you are not!

God, in His marvelous wisdom, knew that you would misuse, abuse and overuse the stress response, so He gave you the ability to *cathart!* God gave you two natural *cathartic* gifts–crying and laughing. No one taught you how to cry or laugh, but they did teach you not to!

Angels can fly because they take themselves lightly.
　　　　　G. K. Chesterton

Chapter Two

There's a Tape Recorder Playing in Your Head

Remember when you were a child. It didn't take much for you to *cathart*. When I was about five or six years old, my dad, my sister and I were on our way home from grocery shopping. Dad was driving, and my sister was in the front passenger seat. I was in the back, leaning over the front seat, eating a handful of cherries.

Dad had told me to be careful with the pits and to hold them in my hand until we got out of the car. I began looking at the small collection of cherry pits in my hand and wondered, "Would they? Wouldn't they?"

I decided that they would. So I proceeded to take one of the cherry pits and place it into my right nostril. Eureka! I was right! The pit was the same size as my nostril. Satisfied with my accomplishment, I tried to dislodge the pit from my nose. It was then that I came upon another law of nature, that two objects of the same size cannot occupy the same space. When I stuck my index finger in my nose to dislodge the pit, I only proceeded to push it further up my nostril. I knew I was in trouble, and it was time to inform Dad.

Dad was pulling the car up in front of the house when I casually mentioned to him, "Daddy, I have a cherry pit up my nose!"

Born To Cathart

He did a double take over the front seat and in a state of shock asked, "You have a ... what? Where?"

Anxiously I repeated, "I have a cherry pit up my nose, and I can't get it out!"

When I showed him how my finger kept pushing the pit upward, this caused him a certain amount of alarm, and he began *catharting*. Actually, he hollered. That started my *catharting*. Actually, I started crying.

My father, in his wisdom, calmed me down and carefully pressed his finger over my left nostril. He told me to blow hard out my right nostril. I did just as he said. That cherry pit flew out of my nostril and ricocheted off the front dashboard into the back seat. I thought I had invented a new kind of pea shooter.

Once the emergency was over, my father dared to ask, "Marion, why did you put a cherry pit up your nose?"

"I wanted to see if it would fit," I replied innocently.

I can only imagine that my father was very happy I wasn't eating a peach!

When you were a child and cut your finger, you ran all the way home to Mommy. When you got to her, Mommy kissed you, cleaned and bandaged your bleeding knee. Then Mommy began to *shush* you. She told to quiet down and stop crying. Depending on your age, Mom stuck in your mouth either a pacifier, a bottle, a cookie or a soda. You heard messages like, "Stop that sniffling! What are you crying about? Wipe those tears out of your eyes!" We have all heard, "You want to cry about something? Get over here! I'll give you something to cry about!"

There was a hidden message which simply said that you're not supposed to cry. Over time, the accumulated effect of those messages began to take its toll. (Actually, you were born with a tape recorder in your mind set on "record.") You have been recording messages about crying and laughing since the womb. Some of you have a tape full of messages that need to be erased.

However, parents were not the only ones responsible for suppressing your cathartic tears. Sometimes, even your friends,

Born To Cathart

television shows or songs you heard taught you that it was not *cool* to cry.

Growing up, I don't think I ever saw Matt Dillon on *Gunsmoke* cry one time, regardless of how bad he got shot up. Miss Kitty and Chester seem to do all the crying. Listening to Dick Clark's *American Bandstand*, I heard songs like "Big Girls Don't Cry." Crying was only for weak individuals, babies, women and sissies. Do you know what happened to all your pain? It went inside and stayed there. Come on, be honest with yourself. You can remember times when you were physically or emotionally hurt, and you did everything you could to prevent the tears from flowing. Isn't it ironic that the same world that told you not to cry is the same world that tells you, "What you need is a *good* cry?"

What is a *good* cry? It is catharting out all your pain and the hurt. A good cry is an emotional cleansing finished with a loud sigh of relief. Where do you go to have a *good* cry today? I once went to a church (not my denomination) because in the back of this church they had a cry room. I went into that area, sat down, and began sobbing with all my heart. A lady came over and tapped me on the shoulder.

She asked me, "What are you doing?"

I told her, "I'm crying!"

"You can't stay here," she replied.

I asked, "Why not? Isn't this a cry room?"

"Yes, but you can't be more than two years of age!" she exclaimed.

Do you see what I mean? After you reach age two, you're not supposed to cry.

The way in which God created us is truly wonderful. Scripture tells us that we are *fearfully and wonderfully made*. (Psalm 137:14) Being single and having my share of frightening dates, I have found myself praying, "God, I have met the fearfully made. Now, could I please meet the wonderfully made?"

Talking about the fearfully made, I was giving a presentation in Dallas, Texas, to a group of single Pentecostals. After the presentation one of the *fearfully made* approached me and shared the fact that I reminded him of his *late* grandmother! I burst into laughter. Somewhat insulted, he reassured me that he meant that as a compliment. I told him, "I know you meant to be nice. I only wish your grandmother could have been alive!"

Say out loud to yourself, "*Hearty is healthy!*" In order for you to cathart, it must be *hearty*! Even though crying is emotionally healing, it never ceases to amaze me how we'll stop ourselves from doing it.

A woman came to see me for counseling. As she began telling me her story, she started crying. I handed her the tissues, and she mumbled, "I'm sorry. I don't mean to cry."

I encouraged her to go ahead and let the tears out. We almost wound up in a knock down, drag-out fight over whether or not she should cry. She kept insisting she couldn't cry because she wouldn't be able to stop. I kept insisting that she could and would stop.

Finally, in desperation she hollered, "What makes you so sure I'll be able to stop?"

Resolutely, I told her, "This session is going to end in about fifty minutes, and after that I'm going home!" Fortunately, she saw the humor in that and laughed.

As a therapist, when someone starts crying in my office, I've learned not to offer them tissues. Every time I do, they cease their crying to say, "Thank you." Then they wind up apologizing for their tears. So, I have learned to let them sit there and cry. (You would be amazed to know the number of people who don't even reach for the box of tissues sitting on the table next to them.)

Those old messages repeat over and over in your mind like tape recordings. They haunt and prevent you from the satisfying feelings of *heartily catharting* out your emotional pain. Julia Cameron, in her book *The Artist's Way*, speaks about how we are "victims to our own internalized perfectionist, a nasty internal and eternal critic, the Censor, who resides in our (left) brain and keeps up a constant stream of subversive remarks that are often disguised

Born To Cathart

as truth." She encourages us to remember that "your Censor's negative opinions are not truth." Ms. Cameron reminds us to "stop taking the Censor as the voice of reason and learn to hear it for the blocking device that it is."

I'm thinking of starting classes, entitled "Cry Your Way To Health"! I believe that people would be lined up at the door waiting to enroll. However, I have devoted myself to the other natural, cathartic release–laughter.

As an infant, just a few weeks old, there came from within you the first of many giggles. It has been said that a normal, healthy four-year-old child laughs, on the average, five hundred times a day. The average adult laughs approximately fifteen to seventeen times a day. What happened to that laughing child? It heard messages like, "Wipe that smile off your face! What do you think is so funny? What are you grinning at?"

You grew up believing that in order to be a mature, responsible adult, you must be very serious! I like the saying that states: *We must have a sense of seriousness to excel in this world, but we must have a sense of humor to survive.* Unfortunately, people are taking life so seriously that it's killing them from the inside out.

Born To Cathart

Born To Cathart

When you laugh, the whole system vibrates,
a dancing diaphragm, dancing cells.
All the cells are happy, and when you are happy,
you have a longer life.
                    Samuel Avital

Chapter Three

Like A Medicine . . .

Thousands of years ago, one wiser than I wrote in the Book of Proverbs (Proverbs 17:22): *A merry heart doeth good like a medicine.* Now, if I am correct, it would still be a complete sentence if the period followed the word *good*. Yet, under the inspiration of God, the writer added, *like a medicine!* Therefore, laughter is medicinal.

Returning late from a out-of-town speaking engagement, I was tired and hungry. Only a fast food restuarant was open at that late hour. I pulled up in front of the menu board and heard a voice over the microphone ask me for my order. "I'll have a cheeseburger, french fries and an Oreo shake. Thank you." The voice repeated my order but announced, "Oh, I'm sorry but our shake machine is down!" Immediately, I responded, "That's okay. I'm a therapist. I can talk to it! There was dead silence as I envisioned the voice looking about in wonder. After a few seconds, I heard, "Mame, you don't understand. Our shake machine is not only down...it's dead!" With that, I screamed, "Oh no! They always wait to late to call the therapist!" When I got to the drive-thru window, the voice handed me my cheeseburger with a very healthy distance between us. Suddenly, I wasn't tired anymore. That little medicinal laugh break was

Born To Cathart

like a shot of B-12.

Under stress, your body will react accordingly. Avoiding all of the medical terminology, when stressed, your body goes into the protective response of fight or flight. Immediately, you become very alert and focused. You become very *intense* when you are stressed. In fact, you get *so intense*, that you even "camp in tents!" (Sorry about that! That was a very poor joke, but I love it!)

What happens when you laugh? Researchers tell us that when you laugh, your heart rate and your blood pressure increase. However, when you stop laughing, your heart rate and blood pressure fall below your norm. Laughter produces endorphins–the body's natural pain killers. It also produces or stimulates the production of chemicals that give you a sense of well being and empowerment. After a good, hearty laugh, you feel relaxed, calm and back in control. Laughter increases your respiration and oxygen exchange, muscular activity and heart rate.

Laughter stimulates the entire cardiovascular system. A hearty laugh is usually followed by a period of relaxation where the heart, respiration and muscle tension return to below normal levels. Have you ever noticed that after a good laugh you can think more clearly? Did you know that when you laugh heartily, you stimulate both hemispheres of your brain, which is the optimum condition for creativity and problem solving? In fact, when researchers analyzed the tears of a hearty laugh, they found that emotional tears carried the same toxins found in cells under stress. Therefore, your body is catharting. It is releasing and purging the toxins your body created under stress.

It has been documented that when you laugh, it helps to boost your immune system. When you're laughing and feeling good, it is difficult to think about getting sick. You don't have time to be ill. Under stress, your immune system gets depressed, and you become subject to all sorts of illnesses and diseases. Stress can make you sick. (Suggested reading: *Why Zebra's Don't Get Ulcers*, by Robert M. Sapolshy.)

Laughter is an intricate part in many rehabilitation and hospital programs. I know of one rehabilitation center in Houston that plays my tape, *Laughing Your Way Through Stress*, for some of their patients. Laughter distracts them from their pain and discomfort. Norman Cousins found that ten minutes of hearty belly laughter gave him two hours of "pain-free" sleep. For this reason, I call laughter the "Great Distracter!"

❋ ❋ ❋ ❋ ❋ ❋ ❋

Laughter is also psychologically good for you. It makes it easier for other people to get along with you. Laughter opens you up to many other positive emotions in life such as faith, love, hope, joy, encouragement and peace. When you smile and laugh, others feel emotionally safe with you. Similarly, when you're under stress, you become tense and emotionally rigid. You don't appear approachable, and, therefore, others avoid you.

Maybe you're thinking thoughts such as, "I don't have any reasons to laugh! You don't know what's going on in my life! That's easy for you to say! You're not going through what I'm going through!" Well, that may be true. And I don't mean to make light of your situation. However, numerous research projects on the physiological and psychological effects of stress have proved that laughter is indeed good for your health.

Norman Cousins, who wrote the book *Anatomy of an Illness*, called laughter an internal jog for the system. Laughter keeps everything moving. I like to tell people that if they laugh heartily every day, they may not have to worry about being constipated. I met a female octogenarian comedienne whose motto is, "Laugh till you leak!" That's my kind of lady! I only pray that I'm laughing and leaking well into my eighties.

In my work with many heart and cancer patients, I have found that those individuals who face catastrophic medical challenges usually display a greater sense of humor. The following are excerpts from the book *Humor and the Health Professions*, by Vera M. Robinson:

Born To Cathart

A group of Hospice patients developed a bumper sticker which read "Hospice, what a way to go."

A patient recovering from heart surgery commented when you wake up you're convinced you didn't make it but you're not sure you made it to Heaven, either.

A cancer patient created a cartoon about the loss of hair following Chemotherapy. A picture of a bald head with one lone hair sticking straight up is captioned, "I just washed my hair and I can't do a thing with it."

A group of patients walking in the woods, one says to the other, "Don't worry, we can always follow our hair back to the camp."

Comedian Steven Allen is a man who thinks funny and who can ad-lib at the most stressful and embarrassing times. He was trying to cope from surgery for colon cancer. He joked his way through hospitalization and helped others around him to cope. He was thinking about doing a musical sketch about his operation. "Just after the doctor has removed part of my colon, I suddenly sit up and look into the camera and sing, 'All of me. Why not take all of me?'"

I said previously that a normal, healthy four-year-old laughs an average of five hundred times a day, and the average adult fifteen times a day. What happened to you? Where did your humor go? Has it been drowned out of you because of life's cares and woes? Or have you bought into the message that life is so serious that now it's killing you?

Not too long ago, I was conducting a workshop in Florida. After completing the seminar, I visited with my father's brother, Uncle Eddie. My uncle, in his eighties now, is still the resident comedian of our family. Upon turning eighty, he told me that if he lives long enough, he will be able to shoot his golf score.

One morning we decided to play some golf. After several holes and numerous jokes, it was my turn to tee off. I got my driver and golf ball and walked reverently to the ladies' tee. With a mighty swing, I can say I drove the ball a good two hundred yards or more. As I walked back to the golf cart, my uncle, in his unique way, looked at me and said, "Marion, have you ever taken golf lessons?"

Thinking that he was about to compliment me on my great drive and form, I replied, "Well, no, Uncle Eddie, I haven't."

"That's a shame," he said. "I know a good lawyer. We could have gotten your money back!"

After he retired from the New York City Police Department, Uncle Eddie worked for the Internal Revenue Service on Long Island. One day, he was attending a mandatory class on fact versus opinion. Typically, around ten o'clock the class would take a coffee and donut break. However, the instructor paid little attention to the time and talked beyond the break point. My uncle kept looking at his watch, and other participants began moving around in their seats, hoping the instructor would take the hints. Yet these obvious cues seemed to go unnoticed by the instructor.

Shortly thereafter, the instructor turned to my uncle and asked, "Mr. O'Connor, we have been talking about fact and opinion. Could you please give me an example of each?"

"Why, yes!" responded my uncle. "It is a *fact* that on the corner of this street there is a donut shop, and it is my *opinion* that if you keep talking, we're going to miss our break!"

Laughter ensued, and the class was dismissed.

Even though one laughs a lot in life, one can still have their share of trials and tribulations. Look at my uncle, and you'll see a man with a wonderful sense of humor. Nevertheless, he, too, has had his share of difficult trials in his life. However, it is has been his sense of humor that has helped him cope with each one.

Psychologically, laughter does wonders for your self-esteem.

Born To Cathart

It is a magnet that draws people to you. People love to be around others who can make them laugh. That was the magnet that drew people to my father. Living with him was like living with "Walter Mitty." Dad could make difficult and uncomfortable tasks a lot easier by spicing them up with humor. Just ask my brother Jack. Here's one of Jack's favorite stories about our Dad . . .

The winter of 1948 was cold. Dad, a New York City Transit Policeman, had taken a side job as a superintendent of an apartment building in Jackson Heights, New York. The outside thermometer read below 32 degrees. The tenants banged on the pipes for more heat. Dad and I went to the basement to stoke the old furnace with coal for the evening. For a teenager, this was not a pleasant task. We began shoveling piles of coal into the belly of the furnace. I started to lag behind in my work, so Dad came up with an idea. He said, "Let's pretend that we're on an ocean liner heading across the Atlantic. We've run into a huge storm which is battering the ship. The captain has called for more speed to fight the angry waves. And more speed means more coal. Only we can save the ship from going down." "More coal!" the captain yells. Together Dad and I shoveled coal into that furnace until the storm ended, and I forgot all about my discomforts.

In the mid-sixties, on a trip back from New Jersey, my brother had received some discouraging news. He and Dad were waiting for the ferryboat to shuttle them back from Staten Island to the Brooklyn side of New York. Jack just stared out the car window pondering his uncertain future. Realizing the discouragement Jack was feeling, Dad distracted him from his thoughts by asking, "Jack? How many cars do you think can fit on that ferryboat over there?"

"I don't know," Jack replied half-heartedly.

Dad continued, "You think maybe fifty?"

Jack now turned his attention to the cars loading on the ferryboat and guessed, "Yeah. Maybe fifty."

"You know, I think it could be more like sixty! What do you think?" continued Dad. Before long, Jack lost his bad mood in the mental challenge of how many cars could fit on a ferryboat. Today, Jack still laughs at how Dad tricked him out of that bad mood.

Born To Cathart

It is a wonderful heritage to come from a laughing family. My father always seemed to have a humorous response on his lips. He died in 1985, but the laughter continues. Peter, my nephew and the namesake of his grandfather, told me one day, "This family should carry around a snare drum and a cymbal!"

When I asked why, he replied, "Because we're the family of the one-liners! Crash, Boom, Bang!"

❋ ❋ ❋ ❋ ❋ ❋

It's impossible for you to laugh and be mad at the same time. Do the following experiment while you're reading this book. Slump your shoulders, put your head down and put a sad look on your face. Now, try to feel happy. Similarly, put your shoulders back, sit up straight, put your head up in the air, a smile on your face and try to feel sad. You can't do it! They are incompatible with one another.

Think of laughter as an oasis in the desert of life. At the oasis, you find shade, refreshment, and renewing. It never ceases to amaze me how people choose to travel the desert without stopping for a long, cool drink from the oasis of laughter.

You were born with the ability to laugh but not with a sense of humor. A sense of humor is cultivated. It's not uncommon to discover that many comedians grew up in dysfunctional homes filled with abuse, alcoholism, drugs, violence and neglect. So how did they get their sense of humor? They developed it! It became their survival technique. They escaped to the oasis of laughter to avoid the hot sun of life's desert.

God, the great physician, has written us a prescription for life. He knew His creation would need the physiological and psychological benefits of laughter to help counterbalance the effects of stress.

However, that tape recorder in your mind keeps playing those negative messages about laughter over and over again. Therefore, at times when you want to release your stress through a little light

Born To Cathart

moment of comic relief, you often stop yourself from laughing. Those messages haunt you and ultimately take the fun out of your life.

When I was a young girl and started goofing off, my parents would express their disapproval by giving me "*the look*"! That *look* said it all! It meant, "Stop what you are doing right now!" Sometimes, I think that adults still give themselves *the look* just to keep themselves in line. Isn't it amazing how we inhibit and neglect this wonderful gift of God?

There is no magic formula to *catharting*. If one merely wants to laugh, all one has to do is laugh! Fake it! Everyone sits around waiting for someone to come up and tell them a joke. The cognitive, rational and logical side of your brain always wants a reason to laugh. Okay! You need a reason! Go weigh yourself. Believe me, standing on that scale, you'll cathart! You'll either start laughing or crying.

I've been told that if one laughs loudly hard and strong for fifteen seconds, it's equal to the cardiovascular effects of hard rowing for three to four minutes or about 100 times. Which would you rather do? As for me, I'm going for the fifteen seconds!

Did you ever notice how much you enjoy laughing when you don't hold yourself back? You will always feel better when you cathart! Use *"I will feel better today if I cathart"* as your daily affirmation.

I'm not so naive as to think that laughter can solve all of your problems. Some of the events that happen in life are difficult and hard to handle. However, it is laughter that helps you find a way through those ordeals.

I am reminded of the late author, UCLA professor, and laughologist Norman Cousins. While Norman was in the hospital battling a life-threatening disease, he had a nurse that drove him crazy. I call them "we" nurses, because they are always wanting to know, "How are *we* doing?"

One particular morning, a "we" nurse came into Norman's room with a specimen cup. "Mr. Cousins? *We* need a urine speci-

Born To Cathart

men. I'll be back in a few minutes!"

On his breakfast tray there was an unopened can of apple juice. Norman opened the apple juice and poured it into the specimen cup and waited. When the nurse returned, she asked, "How did *we* do?"

Norman held the cup up high and said nothing.

She took one look at it and remarked, "My! My! My! Aren't *we* a little bit cloudy this morning?"

Norman agreed with her and said, "I think so, too. So here, let me run it through again!" Then he proceeded to drink the apple juice.

Can you imagine the look on that nurse's face? As funny as that story is, it did nothing to change that nurse. However, it did help to change Norman. I imagine he laughed every time he told his practical joke on that "we" nurse with every one of his visitors.

Laughter may not change your problems. It changes *you* in those problems. It energizes, empowers, refreshes, renews and brightens your life to help you through those problems.

Do you believe that the God of all creation would give us such a beautiful gift as laughter to be used only now and then? I think God wants us to laugh multiple times each day. Come on, let that left brain of yours relax. Let it take a break. The Bible says you were created in His image. Personally, I think God is a laughing God.

In the Book of Genesis, it says that God *worked* for six days and rested the seventh. Do you really envision God slaving away behind some big, oak desk trying to meet heavenly deadlines? Did God have his own little *Dilbert* cubicle? Did He punch the clock working fourteen to sixteen hours a day trying to create the world? Was there overtime? So, when He finally finished, He took a day off?

That's not the way I picture it. I think God was having fun up in heaven creating all creatures great and small. When you read through the creation story, you will find times when God sits back, admires His work and says, "It is good!" Finally, when He

Born To Cathart

finished, God stepped back and proclaimed, "It is *very* good!" I think He gave all His angels high-fives!

Imagine God up in heaven ready to create man and woman and turning to His angels and stating, "Let's give these humans something that's fun. Something that will help them bear the weight of the world. Let's call that fun thing . . . *LAUGHTER!*"

If I gave someone a precious gift and they tossed it aside unused, I'd be upset. Did you ever stop to wonder if God is sometimes offended when His children fail to use His gift of laughter? That's why my mission is life is *to resurrect laughter in the lives of individuals in a stressful world!* I like to think of myself as the Don Quixote of laughter, chopping down the windmills of seriousness.

> Jesus,
> I believed you laughed
> As Mary bathed you
> And Joseph tickled your toes.
> I believe you giggled
> As you and other children
> Played your childhood games.
>
> And when you went
> To the Temple
> And astounded the teachers,
> I believed you chuckled
> As all children chuckle
> When they stump adults.
>
> And surely there were
> Moments of merriment
> As you and your disciples
> Deepened your relationship.

Born To Cathart

And as you and Mary
And Martha and Lazarus
Fellowshipped, mirth
Must have been mirrored
On your faces.

Jesus,
I know you wept
And anguished. But
I believe you laughed, too.
Create in me
The life of laughter.

—Lois H. Morgan

Born To Cathart

Born To Cathart

How do you spell "relief"?
L-A-U-G-H!
    Rev. Dennis O. Rinehart

Chapter Four

But? What If I...?

The *what if's*! They'll scare the living daylights out of you. Many times you'll stop yourself from laughing because you're afraid that your laughter will hurt you or someone else. It is true that laughter has been used to hurt, to shame and to ridicule. Sarcastic laughter erects walls between people. It separates rather than unifies. However, the laughter that I am speaking of comes from a source of pure joy, health and love. This kind of laughter brings people together. Victor Borge, the Danish pianist, is credited with the statement that "the shortest distance between two people is a smile." I believe that would also include a good, healthy laugh.

Being able to laugh at yourself or something outside of yourself, which is not directed at hurting someone, helps to unite people. Laugh with me, and I have found another soul-mate, friend and playmate.

In my travels around the United States, I find that people are afraid to really let go and belly laugh. I conducted an informal survey of two hundred people on laughter at a local Houston cardiovascular center. When I tallied the answers, the overwhelming results clearly indicated that the majority of individuals felt that laughter should be a part of one's work environment, home

Born To Cathart

and health care and that laughter should be utilized by employers, employees, spouses, parents, doctors and nurses. However, the results also indicated that humor, except perhaps in the home, was not being utilized as a stress reliever. Why? The overwhelming fear of offending someone. Sounds like some old messages to me, "Stop that laughing! That's not nice."

Let's face it. There are going to be times when your attempts at humor will fail, and you will fall flat on your face. Let's say that out of one hundred attempts at using laughter to lighten a tense situation, you fail twenty times. Please, don't sacrifice the other eighty positive humorous interventions. If you unintentionally hurt, you can always say, "I'm so sorry!"

Read the following letter written by an anaesthesiologist taken from the book *Humor and The Health Professions*, by Vera M. Robinson, which illustrates that sometimes our laughter will be misunderstood.

"You saw me laugh after your father died. I was splashing water on my face midway between the emergency room lobby and the far green room where his body lay. Someone told a feeble joke and I brayed laughter like a donkey, decorum forgotten until I met your glance over the physician's gray flannel shoulder— your eyes streaming with tears. To you I must have appeared as a callous buffoon in green pajamas. A personification of all that is cold and impersonal about hospitals. In silence, I dried my face on paper towels, rough as a sackcloth, and retreated to the opening. My laugh was inappropriate, and for that I apologize. But it was, nonetheless, a necessity . . . From training and experience we learn to erect emotional defenses . . . Where we may appear emotionless behind our various masks please understand: much of the stress that health care workers suffer comes about because we do care. We cared about your father . . . All of us worked really hard. We intubated, oxygenated, monitored, massaged, shocked, injected and in our own ways, we prayed. Nothing helped . . . Confronting death as frequently as we do in hos-

Born To Cathart

pitals causes us to weight the scales with sorrow. We are left to search out our own sources of counterbalancing joy . . . The most universal, inexpensive, egalitarian, legal, and portable source of joy is laughter. Being human, and consequently clumsy jugglers, we will all sooner or later laugh at the wrong time. I hope your father would understand that my laugh meant no disrespect. It was a grab at balance. The malignance is what physiologists call a righting reflex–what happens when a cat is thrown into the air. That day you saw me laugh, I knew that another patient was waiting who needed my care and full attention in surgery. As I stood at the sink and washed sweat and vomitus from my face and arms, my laugh was no less cleansing for me than your tears were for you. Mea culpa."

Laughter . . . "the most universal, inexpensive, egali-tarian, legal and portable source of joy." Yes!

✻ ✻ ✻ ✻ ✻ ✻

Would you believe that people are afraid to heartily laugh? In order to heartily laugh you must be willing to give up the C word–CONTROL! This fear of hearty laughter is tied directly to your ego. You don't want to cathart because . . . **CATHARSIS IS SLOPPY!**

Just think about physical catharsis. There's nothing pretty or neat about it! But that didn't stop you from releasing, purging and letting go the last time you were nauseous. When your mind sent a message to your stomach to reverse gears, you *catharted*, and you did so heartily. *HEARTY IS HEALTHY!* The heartiness of catharting scares you. You are uncomfortable with yourself or anyone who has the freedom to release, purge or let go. I attend a United Pentecostal Church where worship can be very demonstrative, very cathartic. It's joy unspeakable and full of glory. However, there are some individuals whom you couldn't pay to attend a church service. Yet, these are the same individuals who think

Born To Cathart

nothing of hooping or hollering over some sporting event. And, they say they're not comfortable with demonstrative worship? People are strange. More respect and homage is given to a pig's skin, basketball or baseball than to our God—Jesus! Doesn't the first commandment say that we are to love Him with our whole heart, mind, soul, and *strength*?

Jesus Christ has done more for my life than any sports hero! What about you?

❋ ❋ ❋ ❋ ❋ ❋ ❋

Let's look at the anatomy of a cathartic laugh. A cathartic laugh is divided into three parts. The first part is the land of controllable, socially acceptable laughter. It is neat and pretty. You could stay here forever. Physically, is it doing your body any good? No!

Dr. Annette Goodheart, Ph.D., from California, believes that our faces have been frozen in one gigantic, socially acceptable expression. The interminable receptionist grin for women and the wall street grin for men. Like your mother always said, "If you keep making a face like that, it's going to freeze that way!" Mom was right!

The second part of a laugh is the land of no return. Here, you're beginning to lose some control, and it frightens you. Therefore, you begin begging and pleading for people to stop making you laugh. Fervently, you try to regain control. You hold your side, face and stomach all in an effort to stop laughing. The infectiousness of laughter is taking effect. Soon, you're in the third part of a hearty laugh . . . the land of uncontrollable, cathartic laughter.

In the land of uncontrollable laughter, all control is gone. Your body is rejoicing. It's celebrating the cathartic process. It won't be long until tears come streaming out your eyes, your nose runs, muscles atrophy and you'll look like you're drunk. You'll be gasping for breath, inhaling and exhaling at rapid speeds. Try to talk,

Born To Cathart

and you find it difficult to speak. It is slob city from now on. It won't be long till the world knows that you are a secret, closet *snorter.*

Desperately, you'll try to regain some form of control but to no avail. Cathartic messages are now being sent from the brain to your lungs. Now you're coughing and hacking as your lungs release, purge and let go. If you're female, your bladder relaxes, and you find yourself sprinting to the rest room. By this time, your ego has shrunk in defeat and embarrassment.

Really, who wants to do this in public? Did you ever stop doing some healthy activity because your ego got in your way? ("Pride goeth before destruction." Proverbs 16:18) You won't ride a bicycle unless you have padded spandex shorts. (Who needs more padding?) You avoid activities because you don't have the right sneakers, equipment, sweat band, warm-ups, T-shirt, gym bag, water bottle or head set. Whatever! They're all excuses! I know because I've used them all myself at one time or another. However, "he who laughs . . . lasts!"

If you were one of my depressed clients and I told you that I wanted you to laugh in your car all the way home from my office, you probably wouldn't do it. Why? If you're like so many people, you'd be afraid of what other drivers would think about you. Do you think the traffic cares whether or not you stay healthy? By "traffic" I mean any person, place or thing that comes into your life. It's all traffic. Honk your horn and move on because those other drivers are not going to come to your funeral to pay their respects. They're not going to stand over your casket and say, "Thanks a lot for not laughing in your car the other day and looking stupid. But, it didn't matter. I wasn't watching."

❋ ❋ ❋ ❋ ❋ ❋ ❋

Another fear about laughter is that it could hurt you professionally. Everyone loves the clown; they just don't promote them. Unfortunately, this is sometimes true. You will find censors all over the place. Censors feel it is their job to stop you from catharting. Catharting makes some individuals uncomfortable. If you cathart, they may start to cathart. And that would mean losing control.

A man, in his mid thirties, attending one of my stress classes told me he gave up laughter for three months. During that time he suffered a heart attack. He attributes his lack of laughter and his willingness to take on all the stress of work as the reasons for his getting sick. I'm not implying that if you stop laughing, you're going to have a heart attack. Given his family history, this man was well on the way to having a heart attack in the near future. He just believes taking on all that stress made it happen a lot sooner than expected.

A group of school administrators and myself participated in an outdoor, experiential training course. The course consisted of numerous mental and physical obstacles that would challenge our ability to communicate effectively as a team. The last challenge of the day was to scale a ten foot wall.

However, I do not wear pants. Until this point, my wearing a skirt had not been a debilitating factor in my accomplishing any of the other obstacles on the course. But now, going over a ten foot wall modestly was a challenge for me and the team. Could we do it? I was reassured . . . "No sweat!"

The team jumped into the project with wild enthusiasm as up and over everybody went except for me. The team cheered its success when they reached the other side of the wall. As we huddled in our process group, the facilitator asked, "Did anyone notice that Marion did not go over the wall?"

Shock registered on the faces of the other team members. How could they have skipped me? This led to an in-depth conversation on how our team could overlook one of its members. The conclusion was that, at times, having a humorous personality was actually a deterrent because the team didn't take those members seriously. By the end of that process group, other school personnel echoed some of the same feelings. The adaptive physical education instructor talked about several times when his input was overlooked because of his casual attire.

It is unfortunate but true that many intelligent, creative individuals are overlooked and underutilized because of their fun-loving personality. Should one give up the humor for the recognition?

In one of my recent workshops, an administrator told the group that he had several employees on his staff who brightened up the office with their humorous personalities. He said, "If they never did another ounce of work, I still wouldn't get rid of them."

When asked why this was so, he told us how their humor brightened and added so much to the overall emotional health of the office. "They're worth their weight in gold," he remarked.

Your humor is gold. Gold will last while the business suits hang in closets and get eaten up by the moths.

❋ ❋ ❋ ❋ ❋ ❋ ❋

Growing up, I suffered a near fatal illness—"foot in mouth disease." It seemed I was always saying the wrong thing at the wrong time. In my early twenties, a friend's mother passed away. Naturally, I went to the funeral home to express my sympathies. Growing up in New York, many of my friends were Italian, and their grief was very demonstrative in its expression. Not being accustomed to people's expressing their grief so openly, I was initially hesitant and frightened when I entered the funeral parlor. Rosie escorted me up to the casket, and we said a short prayer. Then, she escorted me over to greet her father, the grieving husband of over fifty years.

When I came face to face with my friend's father, all I could utter in the midst of all his Italian was, *"I'm so sorry!"* From there, I greeted all the relatives. I met the deceased's children, sisters, brothers, nieces, nephews and every one of her grandchildren. With each introduction, I kept repeating, *"I'm so sorry!"*

Finally, left alone, I wandered to the back of the parlor to sit down and rest from all my *so sorrying*! My plan was to stay only a little while and then make a graceful exit. However, just before I was about to leave, a daughter of the deceased whom I had not seen before came and sat down next to me. We spoke not a word to each other, and the awkward silence hung loudly between us. It was then that I turned to her and called her by name. Once again, the heavy blanket of silence laid itself upon our shoulders, at least, on mine. I felt I should say something. So, I turned to her and in my inevitable, foot-in-mouth way asked, "So, what's new?"

Shock registered on our faces immediately. What had I said? The pitiful, grieving daughter just stared at me and then pointed to her mother's casket. I quickly rebounded by saying, "Oh, yeah! I'm so sorry!" This time I swallowed my foot so far down my throat I wound up with a severe case of athletes' mouth. Try to explain that to your doctor!

If I gave up attempting to be humorous because I was afraid of hurting someone, I would be giving up one of the greatest gifts that God has for His children. Fortunately, I have recovered from my *disease* significantly enough to become the George Jessel of our family funerals.

Born To Cathart

Show me a patient who is able to laugh and play, who enjoys living, and I'll show you someone who is going to live longer.
           Bernie Siegel, M.D.

Chapter Five

Appreciators and Presenters

A sense of humor can be manifested in two ways. One can be either a presenter or an appreciator. Afterall, what is laughter? It is a thought you think that is manifested in a hearty ha-ha! I spoke recently at a local service organization. After my presentation, a young man came up to me and stated rather proudly, "Lady, I just want you to know that I am a *hard* audience! It takes a lot to get me to laugh. But you made me laugh. Lady, you're good!"

How sad it is to have this kind of attitude. Being a *hard* audience hurt only this young man, not me. After all, I don't make people laugh. People make themselves laugh by the thoughts they think about what they see and hear. Afterall, what is laughter? It is a thought you think that is manifested in a hearty ha-ha! It would have been better for this young man to say that he was an *easy* audience, that is, a person who appreciates humor and willingly laughs easily.

What are you doing when someone is telling you a joke? You're thinking. All the time a joke is being told to you, you are thinking about what is being said and what makes it so funny. That's why you immediately laugh when you get to the punch line. If you interpret the joke to be funny, it will be. If you think the joke is stupid and makes no sense, you'll probably not laugh.

Here's a joke. Remember: Think.

A man has 100 bricks to build a fireplace. He

only uses 99 bricks. What did he do with the extra brick?
He threw it out the window!
Did you laugh? Was it funny? No? Okay, let me try another one.

A man is riding a subway train smoking a big old cigar. The train is very crowded, and there's no place for him to sit. However, he sees a rather fashionable, elderly woman sitting in a seat with her French poodle sitting on the seat next to her.

The man tells the woman, "Lady, move that dog. I want to sit down."

She exclaims, "That seat is for Fifi."

"Lady, move the dog. I want to sit down!" he yells.

"No! That's Fifi's seat!" she insists.

"Lady, move the dog, or I'll throw her out the window," he threatens.

"No! This seat is for Fifi!" she declares.

With that, the man picks up her dog, Fifi, and throws her out the subway car window. The woman then yanks the cigar from the man's mouth and throws it out the window.

They both get off at the next stop and look down the tracks to see what happened to the dog and the cigar. To their surprise, they see little Fifi running down the tracks. And guess what she has in her mouth?

The cigar?

No! The brick!

This joke illustrates that humor is in the ear of the beholder and that appreciators have finely tuned ears. If you are like most people, you didn't laugh at the joke about the man and the fireplace. In fact, you probably forgot all about the brick when you began reading the second joke. However, you may have chuckled when instead of the cigar in the dog's mouth, it was that brick you had forgotten about. The people who always seem to appreciate that joke are the appreciators. They jump at every opportunity they can get to laugh.

Born To Cathart

�֍ �֍ ✶ ✶ ✶ ✶ ✶

Sometimes, I get nervous suggesting humor as a way to alleviate stress simply because so much of today's humor is vulgar. The Internet offers many joke web sites where you can pick the kind of humor you like. You can find everything from X-rated to G-rated humor on-line. However, X-rated or sex related humor is still number one in many comedic routines. Fortunately, there are good, funny Christian comedians out there. While it is true that you have to look high and low to find humor that would be considered clean, it is there, and it's worth the search. (See bibliography: *Holy Humor*.)

✶ ✶ ✶ ✶ ✶ ✶ ✶

The presenter of humor is the one who tells the stories and funny jokes. However, humor can be presented in other ways. Teachers who dress up on every holiday are presenters. On Halloween, teachers adorn themselves with pumpkin earrings and vests. When it's Christmas, you'll see them wearing jingle bells everywhere. On Valentine's Day, they are one massive beating heart.

There are many different ways to present humor.

1. *Cut out funny stories and share them with others.*
2. *Collect funny cartoons or cartoon books.*
3. *Visit novelty stores and collect different types of humorous props. (Groucho glasses, clown noses, etc.)*

To be a presenter, you must be willing to take risks. As presenters, we are always faced with the possibility that people might not laugh or appreciate our humor. I encourage presenters to practice their humor on their friends and family. Get a feel for what works and doesn't work. Recently, I made an audio tape of five minutes of laughter. Immediately, I played that tape to a good

Born To Cathart

laughing friend of mine. I figured if she didn't laugh, no one would.

Certainly, it's tough to stand there while people stare and say, "I don't get it!" It's a lonely feeling, but it only lasts for a short time. And it doesn't happen that often. So go for the laughs. Take the risks. The payoffs are great.

If you choose to be an appreciator, all you have to do is open your mouth and laugh heartily. Be playful. *DON'T BE A CRITIC!* If there is one thing we don't need, it's more critics. Appreciators are the ones who usually do the decorating for parties and know the name of every good presenter in the area. Most of my speaking engagements come about as the result of appreciators. They are the ones who attend my workshops, go back to their businesses, and recommend me to their supervisors.

If you don't want to be in the limelight as a presenter, develop your ability to be an appreciator. The rewards are just as great. Of course, you can be both an appreciator and a presenter. Personally, I love to be in the audience appreciating other presenters just as much as I enjoy presenting. I get a "double" blessing this way.

※ ※ ※ ※ ※ ※

Has someone taught you not to laugh? Well, you can teach yourself to laugh. Overcome the messages of your past. Put that tape recorder on re-record. Become the comedian you've always wanted to be. There are basically three elements that can make something funny: exaggerations, reversals and surprises. Remember Candid Camera? What made that show so funny? Those three elements. Watching normal reactions of people caught in Candid Camera moments had the viewing audience in stitches. A car suddenly becomes a boat, mailboxes talk to you, and hands come out of the walls to steal food off a table.

If you want to develop a healthier sense of humor, begin looking for these three elements—exaggeration, reversals, and surprises—in your everyday world. The following are a few helpful hints:

Born To Cathart

1. *Keep logbooks of your findings. Record every funny bumper sticker, radio commercial, billboard and sign.*
2. *Collect the unusual and bizarre personal ads from newspapers. The things people say about themselves can be really funny.*
3. *Hang out at your local mall. Watch people in their natural habitat! Human behavior is funny.*

You'll see teenagers with their pants hanging down around their knees. I tell my audiences that I am really worried about today's teenagers and drugs. I think the drugs they are taking are deteriorating their bones, especially their hip bones. Why? They can't keep their pants up! And, what do you think about their purple hair, Mohawks and body piercing?

4. *Read and collect cartoons.*
5. *Create a humor library at home. Explore the humor section at your local bookstore.*
6. *Buy humorous audio books and tapes. Feast yourself on funny and humorous material every opportunity that comes your way.*
7. *Buy joke books. Practice telling some of those jokes to your friends and family.*
8. *Learn a joke a week and tell that joke to ten people. Record their reactions and which jokes got you the biggest responses. Subscribe to Reader's Digest and memorize one joke a month from Laughter is the Best Medicine.*
9. *Ask people to tell you their favorite jokes. If you've heard it before, pretend you haven't and practice your laughing.*
10. *Go hear a Christian comedian. Contact your local Christian bookstore or radio station for information regarding concerts, etc.*

Implement some of these suggestions, and it won't be long before you're manifesting more humor in your life. Refuse to allow your past to censor your future. Remember, life is not a dress rehearsal–make it count!

Born To Cathart

Born To Cathart

You know you sometimes think
yourself into unhappiness, into depression.
Do you know that you can also think yourself into gladness?
It is by such thinking that you get well,
that you prosper, that your prayers are always answered.
                    Albert E. Cliffe

Chapter Six

Ten Irrational Beliefs About Laughter

In the book *A New Guide to Rational Living*, by Albert Ellis, Ph.D., and Robert A. Harper, Ph.D., ten irrational beliefs that underlie our behaviors are discussed. I would like to look at laughter from this perspective and entitle this: "The Ten Irrational Beliefs About Laughter!"

Irrational Belief No. 1: *People must laugh and approve all my attempts at laughter.*

This thought is irrational because not everybody is going to find you or your jokes amusing. Everyone has a different idea of what is or isn't funny. You do not need anyone's approval. You may *want, desire, or prefer* that people laugh at your jokes and funny stories, but wants, preferences and desires do not constitute needs. If someone does not appreciate your humor and criticizes you, protect yourself by thinking:

1. Well, Jerry didn't seem to like my joke about the man and the frog, but Eddie liked it. So I can share my jokes with Eddie from now on.

2. Jerry may not like those kinds of jokes, but I do. And I find them enjoyable.

Born To Cathart

Take the *musts* out of your thinking. It is not a dire necessity that everyone that you tell a joke to laughs. If fifty percent of the people laugh, you're doing well.

Irrational Belief No. 2: *I must be a thoroughly competent and adequate joke teller to be funny.*

You're afraid to tell a joke, funny story or do something humorous because of your fear of failure. You may think failure is the worst of all situations. Remember, virtually no one can be a perfect or competent comedian all the time. Not even some of our greatest comedians hit home runs every time they're on stage. There is always the possibility that, right in the middle of their funniest joke, they flub a line. Everyone has weak points, imperfections and makes mistakes. Your ability to tell a joke is not a definition of your intrinsic value or worth. It's true that you may feel better if they laugh at your jokes, but feeling good does not make you a better person. Practice makes things better. Therefore, I do advise you to practice your delivery in telling a joke. Start telling jokes to your close friends and family members before you become the center of attention at the next party. Join local speaking clubs in your community. I believe that you can improve your performance level although you will never become thoroughly adequate, competent or achieve perfection.

Irrational Belief No. 3: *When people don't laugh at my jokes, then they are horrible, terrible people and should be punished.*

Blaming or condemning people for not appreciating your sense of humor is wasted mental and physical energy. Based on past experiences, people have many ideas of what is and what is not funny. Getting angry at someone because they don't appreciate your attempts at humor is taking on a very selfish, whiny and self-centered attitude. You're not going to receive one hundred percent approval. And by blaming or condemning, you only hurt yourself. Behind this belief is the thought that when people don't laugh, it's the most horrible, terrible and catastrophic thing that could ever happen to you. Which leads us to irrational belief number four.

Irrational Belief No. 4: *If people don't laugh at my jokes, it's awful, horrible and catastrophic.*

I have to admit it's not pleasant or comfortable when people don't laugh with you. But you could protect yourself from getting all bent out of shape by thinking:

1. *I don't like it when I tell a joke at which no one laughs, and they stare at me. But getting all upset about it doesn't change the outcome.*

2. *I didn't get the response I wanted. Let me see how I could change the joke or story to make it funnier.*

3. *I can learn to accept the fact that sometimes people will or will not laugh at my jokes.*

In order for someone's silence not to bother you, you must talk to yourself about the situation to avoid being upset or angry. In order to have more manageable feelings and behaviors, you will need to fine tune your thinking. The whole idea behind rational, cognitive therapy is that your own irrational beliefs upset you.

Irrational Belief No. 5: *I must be happy in order to laugh.*

It's a physiological reaction that when you laugh you will feel happier. Speaking at M.D. Anderson Cancer Center, I met some really wonderful and courageous people. At the close of my presentation, *Laughing Your Way Through Stress,* patients usually come up to share some of their own personal insights. One little lady, originally from the country of India, with a beautiful smile told me that when she enters the hospitality room at the center, the volunteers greet her with, "Here's Mrs. Brownsville! Mrs. Brownsville!"

Born To Cathart

"I'm not Mrs. Brownsville," she states. And with that, she whips off her wig and exclaims, "I'm Mrs. Clean! Mrs. Clean!" What a lady!

At the same presentation, I also met a retired executive from a major oil company. He told me that he had traveled the world all over and now was at the center because he had prostate cancer. Having prostate cancer made him wonder how God designed the human body. He concluded that God must have consulted with engineers. Yes, God consulted with mechanical engineers to design the muscles, nuclear engineers to design the brain, and chemical engineers to design the circulatory system. However, God consulted with those civil engineers to design the waste system, for only a civil engineer would put a water waste line through a recreational area!

Although the two incidents caused me to blush with embarrassment, these people's method of dealing with this terrible illness taught me a valuable lesson that day. You don't have to be happy in order to laugh. When they were able to trap me unknowingly with their humor, they proved once again that the cancer was not controlling their spirits; it only controlled their bodies. And when I joined in their laughter, I celebrated with them the power of the human spirit to overcome adversities through the power of laughter.

You see, there's nothing happy about cancer, chemotherapy, hair loss, nausea and the possibility of death. Yet these two individuals and so many more have taught me that you can find that oasis of laughter in any desert. It is laughter that empowers you to get through difficult events. Don't wait to be happy. Create it now.

When giving another speech at M.D. Anderson Cancer Center, I inquired about the gentleman and his condition. I found out that his cancer is inactive. He likes to say, "The dragon still sleeps!" Did laughter bring about this wonderful happening in his life? Well, it didn't hurt it! Like Norman Cousins, both of these cancer patients used laughter to help them cope with their medical problems. I'm not sure what the outcome has been for the lady from India. If she's still with us, I believe she is somewhere pulling off her wig and laughing.

Irrational Belief No. 6: *All laughter must be spontaneous.*

You plan almost every facet of your life. From the time you get up till the time you go to bed, you are planning. When was the last time you planned to have a good laugh? Most individuals feel that laughter must be spontaneous. However, laughter can be planned. It does not have to be like canned laughter that you might hear during a television sitcom program. Planned laughter means taking your calendar book and scheduling times when you can laugh. Take laughing luncheons with friends. Start that business meeting off with a few jokes or stories. Plan an evening with your laughing friends. Integrate laughter into your life, in some form or fashion, every day.

Recently, one of the top comedians here in the United States decided to call it quits after nine years of a long running television comedy. It's amazing how many people got together to watch that last episode together. What did they do the rest of the nine years?

I remember attending a humor seminar on the night that Johnny Carson was ending his reign as the King of the nighttime talk shows. At about eleven o'clock when Johnny was coming on, everyone at the workshop decided to stay and watch the final episode. Me? I left. I haven't had a TV in my home for the last eighteen years. I don't like it, and I don't rely on a weekly TV program to make me happy. I've learned to create my own happiness.

If you can plan those kind of evenings, then you can plan fun times throughout the whole year. I believe if people threw out their televisions altogether, they would find a lot more things to make them happy. I blame TV for my not being married today. I learned about men from television ads. I learned that most men suffer from indigestion, bad breath, excessive perspiration, rough hands, big feet, arthritis, intestinal distress and iron-poor blood.

Born To Cathart

They have receding hair lines, short tempers, chronic fatigue, dull eyes, headaches, bad skin, constipation and excess fat. Who would want to put up with all that?

You could invite people to a humor party. Tell them to come dressed as their favorite clown or comedian. Do funny skits. Someone act out Abbot and Costello's "Who's on First, What's on Second." If you plan it, you can do it.

I do seminars in many school districts across the United States just to help teachers have a laughing classroom. Did you know there's research that proves that test grades improve when the atmosphere of the classroom is pleasant and humorous? Laughter is a great way to deal with test anxiety. (Of course, you have to study for the test beforehand.)

In order to have a laughing office, home or classroom, you will have to plan. Laughter does not have to be spontaneous. Sure, it's great when it happens that way, but why wait?

Irrational Belief No. 7: *One must be born with a sense of humor.*

Remember this: You were born with the God-given, natural ability to laugh. No one taught you how to laugh. When you were just a few weeks old, out of your belly came a little giggle, a little ha-ha, and the world rejoiced. Yet ever since that time, you've been hearing messages that told you not to laugh. "This is not funny. What are you laughing at? Stop all that foolishness. Wipe that smile off your face."

A sense of humor is something that can be developed and cultivated. As I said earlier, regardless of your upbringing, you can teach yourself to have a better sense of humor. Listen to comedians and notice the inflection in their voices. To and from work listen to their tapes and practice telling the jokes like them. You can be another George Burns. Flood yourself with humorous material. If you want to cultivate a better sense of humor, you could do it by being either the appreciator or the presenter. If you need it, find a laughing role model. Hang around and copy them. Read articles and subscribe to funny magazines. Don't use the excuse, "I just wasn't born with a sense of humor." Well, nobody was! If you weren't fortunate enough to have family members in your life that taught you how to laugh, you can still develop this quality on your own.

Irrational Belief No. 8: *Trying to be funny can be a dangerous and fearsome task and is better to be avoided.*

If you stop and think about it, there are risks in just getting up in the morning, risks in just breathing and living. What kind of a life is a life without healthy risks? When you think about getting in your automobile and driving to work, there's a greater risk in losing your life than in telling a joke. The worst thing that can happen if you tell a joke is that people won't laugh and you'll be embarrassed. Embarrassment can't kill you. In fact, embarrasssment can be a great source for anecdotes for future humorous stories. Yet you can die in an automobile accident on the road. You've got to get away from the mistaken belief that if you can't do it perfectly, confidently and adequately, then you won't do it at all. Remember, if you mess up, you can always say my two famous words, "I'm sorry." So go ahead and take some laugh risks today. Tell someone a joke. Dare to heartily laugh out loud.

Irrational Belief No. 9: *It's all my fault if people don't laugh. I must have done something wrong to cause this failure.*

This is a very powerful irrational belief. It is almost like saying that you're God and what you do or what you don't do affects other people in such a way that you control them rather than their controlling themselves. If I do something and you get mad, I didn't make you mad. You chose to be mad by your own thoughts. It's true that my behavior could have been irresponsible or annoying. And I need to take responsibility for my actions. But you need to take responsibility for your own thoughts about my actions. The words *all, must, can't,* or *should* need to be taken out of your vocabulary.

Born To Cathart

On a Saturday morning, I presented an all day workshop. In order to qualify for continuing education credits, everyone needed to stay the complete eight hours. A small group of fifteen people came dragging into the room. They looked sleepy and not in a mood to laugh. The room being too warm didn't help.

I thought I had presented the workshop much like all my others. However, no matter what I did that day, getting those participants to laugh was a chore. I beat up myself the whole day saying things like, "It's my fault that they're not having a good time. It's my fault they're not laughing." At the end of the day I reviewed the evaluations. Everyone rated me very favorably, but it was the last evaluation that really got my attention. The individual had written, "I would have been more into the class had I not had a hangover." When I read that, I just sat back in my chair and laughed. I had beaten up myself all day long, blaming and condemning myself for what I thought was a lousy seminar. All the while, they're sitting there with a hangover. Based on that information, they wouldn't have enjoyed it even if Bill Cosby was the presenter. Let's bring it down to reality. Don't accept all the credit when things go wrong nor when things go right!

Irrational Belief No. 10: *I can be happy by just sitting back, doing nothing and letting other people entertain me.*

Humans rarely feel happy or alive when they are just sitting back doing nothing except maybe for short periods of rest between their jobs or different types of exertions. There is something about the human nature that we get bored and listless when we just sit around doing nothing all the time. People have to be involved in activities, and they have to feel alive and happy. Anybody who has a reasonable amount of intelligence wants to be absorbed in an activity that makes them feel energetic and part of society. We are goal oriented people. We like to be part of the project. We like to be achieving goals as we go through our everyday life. People who choose to be inert, lazy, or passive and are willing just to sit back and not be actively involved in life and laughter usually lead

Born To Cathart

very flat, dull, unhappy lives. Get involved. Be an appreciator or a presenter. If you're going to be a couch potato, at least laugh out loud when you get the chance. Don't be one to sit on the sidelines and watch the parade of life go by. March along with all the other clowns.

Born To Cathart

Born To Cathart

*A person without a sense of humor
is like a wagon without springs,
jolted by every pebble in the road.*
                          Henry Ward Beecher

Chapter Seven
Laughter and Other Emotions

I said before that laughter may not change your situation, but it certainly can change you in the situation. Some of the more uncomfortable feelings that human beings experience are depression, anger and fear. Laughter can be the distraction that helps you cope with these three uncomfortable emotions.

In the book *Anger Kills*, by Doctors Redford and Virginia Williams, the statement is made, "*Anger kills but will it kill me?*" They report that 20% of the general population has levels of hostility high enough to be dangerous to their health. Another 20% has very low levels, and the rest of the population falls somewhere in between. The kind of anger they're talking about is not the anger that drives people to shoot, stab or kill somebody; it is the everyday sort of anger, annoyance and irritation that courses through the minds and bodies of many otherwise perfectly normal individuals. Getting angry for some people is like taking a small dose of a slow acting poison every day of your life, and the result is often the same. Not tomorrow, perhaps, or even the day after but sooner than most of you would wish, hostility is likely to harm your health.

It is as if anger is your everyday companion. What happens physiologically when you get angry? The authors relate the fact that anger is a toxin to your body. Physiologically, your heart rate and your blood pressure go up. You have massive adrenalin surges flooding your body. The body goes into the protective response of flight and fight. Your breathing becomes rapid and shallow. The immune system goes on hold. Cortisol, a stress hormone, is pouring into your blood stream, having an amplified effect on your heart and arteries. As the angry thoughts and feelings continue, your heart also continues to pump out blood far in excess of the needs of your body. You feel like your heart is going to jump out of your chest. Your head and heart start to pound, and your palms become sweaty. Breathing becomes deep and rapid. All of these physiological signs reinforce the idea that a "real" danger must be close at hand when in reality someone just cut you off on the highway.

Yet it doesn't stop there. Blood pressure rises quickly. Platelets begin to clump in your arteries, and plaque begins to build up and multiply. Adrenalin stimulates your fat cells to empty into your blood stream to provide you with energy and the effort that you would need to exert if this was a real emergency. However, because you are not burning up your fat in order to escape from a real danger and you are just sitting there fuming in your car, your liver converts the fat into cholesterol. What does all this mean? It means that if this situation continues, it can get so big that it could endanger your life. You could become one of the 500,000-plus Americans who have a heart attack each year. So how does laughter help?

Doctors Williams and Williams recommend humor and laughter as one of the strategies to overcome anger. The type of humor they recommend is not ridicule or sarcasm. If you use humor in this manner, it will only cause you to become more aggressive and will not help you. The healthiest type of humor–and the best place to start–is to be able to laugh at yourself. Remember that you cannot laugh and be angry at the same time. They are incompatible. Try laughing and hollering at the same time. You can't do it! In order for you to be angry, you've got to stop laughing. If you can't laugh at yourself, go get a funny tape. Learn to distract yourself. The time it takes to listen to a funny tape is just enough time for you to think thoughts that will calm you and help you reassess

Born To Cathart

your situation.

The physiological effects that this kind of anger has on the human body makes you stop and think, "Do I really want to do this to myself?" My father used to say, "Pick your battles carefully!" The older I get, the more I appreciate the wisdom behind this saying. When you're young, everything is a battle. Of course, when you're young, you think you're going to live forever and you are superman/woman. Go ahead! Fight every battle that comes your way, and it won't be long before you're visiting the doctor's office because of stress related problems. It is a wise person who can stand back and assess a situation asking, "Is it really worth my getting all upset about?"

Laughter puts a bridge between the situation and you. It's your buffer zone. Your oasis. It reminds me of the Quaker farmer who was milking a cow that demonstrated a very mean temperament. After much frustration and knowing his anger was rising within, he addressed the cow, "Thou knowest that I am a Quaker and cannot strike thee in anger and cannot curse thee, but what thou doth not knowest, cow, is that tomorrow I am going to sell thee to a Baptist, and he's going to beat thee with a rod."

I like what Doctors Williams and Williams have to say about anger and how to talk yourself out of it. If you find yourself being cynical, angry or aggressive, they suggest that you ask yourself these questions: (1) "Is the matter worth my continued attention?" If the answer is *yes*, then you'll ask yourself a second question: (2) "Am I justified?"

If the answer to the first question is *no*, they suggest you reason with yourself to short cut your anger. If you can't talk yourself out of that anger or fine tune your thoughts to lower your anger, then try to deflect or distract your anger by using humor.

If you answered *yes* to both questions, then you need to go on to the third question, "Do I have an effective response?" If the answer is *no*, again try to reason with yourself to short circuit your anger.

If you do have an effective response, they encourage you to

Born To Cathart

assert yourself in that situation. I often ask my clients, "Is thinking this way, even if it's true, going to get you what you want?"

Some of the exercises mentioned in *Anger Kills* in regard to using humor to deflect your anger are:

1. *Try to exaggerate the importance of the situation and yourself.*

2. *Play with your untrue sense of doom or your untrue sense of self-importance.*

3. *Be actively applying whimsy. You can substitute a new imagined reality.*

4. *Entertain yourself with puns and double entendres. You can favorably compare your present plight with an exaggerated undesirable situation.*

You're using your brain power to think of funny ways of twisting around your upsetting event so that, instead of producing angry thoughts, you produce more humorous thoughts.

If you're an angry person, then you may be used to being angry and responding in an angry manner. You get so wrapped up in your anger that you miss countless opportunities to enjoy laughter. Many people have to practice allowing themselves to experience the enjoyable, pleasurable feeling of laughter. Pick your battles carefully, and you will see the futility of your own anger. Once you do, you will be more able to come up with different humor inducing devices to deflect your anger.

✳ ✳ ✳ ✳ ✳ ✳ ✳

What about depression? When people come to me for counseling, I usually find that their depression is related to situational or circumstantial dilemmas. In other words, there is some person, place or thing that is frustrating, upsetting, irritating, annoying, or hurting them in some way. In most cases, the individuals are upsetting themselves with their own thoughts about the situation. If you learn to dispute your own irrational thoughts and replace them with more rational and logical ones, you will have more manageable and comfortable feelings.

Several years ago, a client came to me with numerous health and emotional problems. The individual was on massive doses of medication. I tried every technique and theory I knew in order to help her overcome and cope with her depression. Having an unhappy home and medical bills to pay beyond her capability didn't help matters. When she came into the office, I got depressed. Finally, I asked her if she watched movies at home.

She told me, "Why, yes! I watched a movie last night."

Excitedly, I asked, "Oh! Really? Which movie?

Her answer revealed to me why some people stay depressed. She replied, "I watched *Schindler's List.*"

How depressed do you want to get? Even for emotionally healthy individuals, *Schindler's List,* would have a depressing effect. It is a shame that many people die disappointed with life. They never saw what lay around the corner or over the hill, just what went down the drain. They majored in depression.

Turn out the lights, sit alone in a dark room, burn scented candles, listen to mood music, and contemplate how bad life really is. Sounds ridiculous, doesn't it? Yet, that's what I did in college when I got situationally depressed. For a little while the drama of my depression was rather entertaining. Fortunately, I didn't stay in that state for very long. It would usually end around dinner time. In actuality, I needed to turn on the lights, make it as bright as possible and listen to uplifting music.

If you find yourself wrapped in the blanket of depression, my suggestion to you is make a list of how an un-depressed person would be acting. Healthy, normal people would be getting up, getting dressed, going out and doing things. You may say that you don't feel like doing anything. If you want to feel normal, then you need to do normal, healthy activities every day to produce the feelings of normalcy. Flooding yourself with humorous materials has an analgesic effect. For a few minutes, you find yourself deflected away from your depression into the glorious throes of laughter.

This poor woman didn't need to feel more depressed by watching sad films. So I began to explore with her who she thought were funny comedians. She identified the comedy pair of Abbott and Costello. I gave her a counseling homework assignment to review three funny Abbott and Costello tapes during that next week. I instructed her to write a synopsis of each one and read it to me at our next session. When she left the office that day, I gave it no more thought.

The following week, upon entering my office she looked much like her old self. When she began telling me about Abbott and Costello, before my very eyes I saw a transformation in this individual. Her eyes started to sparkle, and she no longer slouched in her chair. I watched as her frown turned into a half smile, to a full grin, and to a hearty laugh.

This transformation lasted the entire fifty minute session. Not long after, she began walking and exercising with her neighbors and began doing more around her house. At the time of this writing, I do not know how this woman is currently doing. I do know that just by listening to or viewing something funny it changed her life and, hopefully, had a lasting effect on her. That's why I say that laughter is like an oasis in the middle of the desert. Depression is like a dry, arid land, but every so often, you come upon this beautiful oasis called laughter. Then it reminds you how wonderful and truly great life really can be.

I told you that I come from a family of good laughers. After my mother died, my father anxiously awaited for his two brothers to arrive at the funeral home to share his grief. Dad knew that when Eddie and Jerry arrived, there would be laughter. And, where there is laughter — there is life.

I remember the night before my Aunt Kay's burial, the fam-

Born To Cathart

ily gathered at the funeral home along with the parish priest, who asked us to relate memorable stories about our loved one. Slowly but steadily, individuals shared beautiful and loving memories of their mother, grandmother, aunt and friend. However, as the stories progressed, they went from the sweet and serious to the sweet and humorous. By the end of the evening, the sound of laughter could be heard echoing from that tiny funeral parlor.

I would hate to think I would have to go through life and face the dry and arid places without having the oasis of laughter as my retreat.

❋ ❋ ❋ ❋ ❋ ❋ ❋

That brings me to the emotion of fear. I am not talking about the kind of fear that comes as a result of the a danger or threat toward your life. I am talking about the fear that is the result of a perceived danger such as talking in front of an audience, asking someone out on a date, the fear of being embarrassed or even writing a book. Laughter can be the method you can use to help deal with the debilitating effects of fear.

President Dwight David Eisenhower got over his fear of public speaking by envisioning his audiences in tattered underwear. This humorous visualization gave President Eisenhower the courage to stand in front of crowds and give speeches throughout his political career. It is important that you can differentiate between healthy and unhealthy fear or anxiety. Ask yourself, "Is this the kind of fear or anxiety that anybody would be experiencing in this situation?"

Also, it is important to differentiate between being uncomfortable and unsafe. If you are in an unsafe situation, then clearly that needs to be avoided. However, you can't avoid all uncomfortable situations and say you're living life to its fullest. Humor in the face of fear can help you regain a sense or feeling of control.

I am reminded of the story of a woman who needed to have a hysterectomy. Her doctor was very professional but, unfortunately, quite aloof. He never smiled or joked with his patient in any way. It was important for her to know that this doctor operating on her was a human being and not a medical machine. The night before her operation, she took a magic marker and wrote across her abdomen, "*No womb in the inn.*" The last thing she remembered before her operation started was seeing her doctor smile as he read those words written across her belly.

A joke about failure may not get you to change your mind about the fear of failing. However, if I could get you to listen to humorous stories or tapes, hopefully, it would distract you from your fear, and you could function better in life. In my cardiovascular classes, I have the patients listen to Bill Cosby's dentist routine. I challenge them to concentrate on their left big toe while they are listening to the twenty minute routine. After a few laughs, that big toe is no longer a thought in their mind. Laughter . . . is the analgesic that you take in order to deal with life's anger, depression and fear.

I remember a time when life was overwhelming me. I was burdened down with fear, doubt and anxiety. As a last resort, I sought the advice and wise counsel of my pastor. (This should have been my first resort.) I've nicknamed him the *Laughing Pastor* because of his great sense of humor.

I visited with him and his wife. We sat down, and I unloaded all of my problems onto his shoulders. He listened intently and advised me on certain areas of concern. After a while, he asked me if I wanted to join them for dinner. Not wanting to go home right away, I decided to join them for the fellowship. As we started for the restaurant, my pastor began to remind me of numerous funny stories and comedy skits I had performed for banquets and fellowship parties at our church. With each memory, I began to laugh and to laugh heartily! I laughed all the way to the restaurant, through the meal, and all the way back to their house. When I got out of the car, I no longer felt any fear, doubt or anxiety for two good reasons. The first reason is that someone had empathetically listened to me. Secondly, I had laughed long, hard

Born To Cathart

and strong for quite some time.

In the time that it took to drive to the restaurant, eat and get back, the *cathartic* effects of laughter had soothed this weary soul. I felt lighter, relaxed, more empowered to face my problems. When my Pastor asked if I wanted to come back into the house and continue talking, I replied, " No, thank you. I'm okay now." Actually, I was better than okay. Once again, *"a merry heart doeth good like a medicine."*

❋ ❋ ❋ ❋ ❋ ❋ ❋

Specifically, what can you do if you find yourself angry, depressed, fearful or anxious because of circumstances in your life? First of all, say out loud to yourself, "STOP!" Then, take a break and get away from the situation. Leave the room or remove yourself from the presence of the problem. Take stock of what you are feeling and thinking. Think about how you want to feel and what you can think to produce those feelings. Thirdly, if you need space, take it. Of course, humor can create that space for you. Instead of pouting or resenting, begin to flood yourself with humorous material. Use humor to distract yourself from the situation you are facing and provide you with the emotional space you need to regroup. If you're still not feeling any better, call up a good laughing friend that you know and say, "Look, I need a laugh break. When can we get together?"

Finally, try to play the game, "So, what if . . .?" For instance, if you are fearful or anxious about speaking in front of a group of people, then ask yourself, "So, what if I . . .?" Then think of everything that can conceivably go wrong. Deliberately catastrophize. Develop responses to those "what if's" in your mind, and you will be better prepared to tackle each one when or if they arise.

The trick is to flood yourself with humorous material on a daily basis. When I teach people techniques to overcome stress, I teach them how to do deep breathing and visualization. These techniques will work to help reduce stress in your life if you prac-

Born To Cathart

tice them often enough. If you only use them every now and then, they won't work as well. It is the same way with laughter. If you take on laughter as an integral part of your everyday life, it will be easier for you to laugh any time it will be easier for you to laugh any time you want.

Do I get angry? Yes. Do I sometimes feel sad and depressed? Yes. Do I get fearful and anxious? Yes. Do I use humor to help cope with those situations? Most definitely. And you can, too. Have fun practicing!

Born To Cathart

Humor might be the soul of wellness.
  Dr. Donald B. Ardell

Chapter Eight

Black Crayons

    I purchased a tee shirt in the theatre district in New York City. On the front was written *"Go For It! Life is not a dress rehearsal!"* This is one my favorite personal slogans. After my parents passed away in 1985 and 1986, I suddenly realized that at 38 years of age, if I lived to be 72 or 73 as my parents had, I had less years to live than I had already lived. If I was going to do anything in life, fulfil any dreams or ambitions, I had better do it now.

    After this revelation, I decided to leave my secure job as a special education counselor for a local Texas school district. I left to pursue my dreams. Even to this very day, I feel a sense of urgency to make every day of my life count. I don't want to get to the end of my life and while I am drawing my last breath say, "I wish I had done this or that." I want to get to the place where I can relinquish life and willingly let it go. Like St. Paul wrote, *"For I am now ready to be offered, and the time of my departure is at hand. I have fought a good fight. I have finished my course. I have kept the faith."* (2 Timothy 4:6-8) Before I leave this world, I want to be able to say I gave the best performance on the stage of life any person could give for God, others and themselves.

    I see myself as a runner in a relay team. Right now, with baton in hand, I'm running the lead. The other runners are waiting for me to pass the baton to them. They're warming up on the sidelines and cheering me on. Yet as our eyes meet, there is a silent communication that speaks, "Now? Is it my turn?"

Born To Cathart

Fortunately, I still have a few laps to go. I haven't done everything that I need to do in life. I haven't run every race. One doesn't get a second shot at this thing called life. So let me run while I can.

You may ask, "Marion, what does this have to do with laughter and stress?" First of all, you've got to wake up every day and purpose in your mind that stress will not have a place in your life. It doesn't matter that I am a psychotherapist; if I don't practice rational, cognitive thinking skills every day, I become just as irrational and illogical as anybody.

You need to discipline your thinking every day. Try asking yourself these three questions when you notice your feelings becoming more uncomfortable and unmanageable:

1. *What am I thinking that is getting me so upset, nervous, anxious or angry?*

2. *Is thinking this way, even if it's true, going to get me what I want?*

3. *What do I want? And what can I think to get more of it?*

As soon as you ask yourself question number one, you immediately stop the upward mobility to more intense, unmanageable feelings. Instead of blaming people, places and things for your being upset, you can accept that it is your own thoughts that are upsetting you. Just by asking this question, you take a step down the staircase of emotions to more manageable, comfortable feelings.

Question number two challenges you to dispute, change or fine tune your thoughts even if these thoughts are true. Not every thought you think will be irrational or illogical. You will think many true thoughts. And you will be right in your anger or hurt. But the real challenge of question two is that it makes you determine what you "really" want. You are the one to decide how you

Born To Cathart

want to feel. Most of us spend too much time trying to change others instead of ourselves.

In the book *Men are from Mars, Women are from Venus*, by John Gray, Ph.D., one of the techniques for resolving problems between couples is the love letter writing technique. I refer my clients to this chapter to help them deal with many of their relationship problems. It starts out with five basic emotions–anger, fear, sadness, regret and love. When you write down your thoughts, it helps to clarify them. However, it is the response letter that I find really helpful. This postscript letter forces the writer to put into concrete, tangible terms the response they would most like to hear or see from the offending party. Without fail, the majority of clients find the response letter harder to write. Which leads us to the third and final question. What do you personally want? And what can you think to get more of it?

Don't tell me what you want someone else to do. Tell me what you want for yourself. Do you want more peace in your life? Do you want more joy in your life? Do you want less stress in your life? When you ask yourself that third question, you force yourself to think about your own desires, wishes and wants. Capturing your thoughts and disputing those that are irrational help you to create more manageable, more comfortable feelings in your life.

Do you want to laugh more in your life? Do you want to have a better sense of humor? Do you want more happiness? Do you want to change those messages of the past? It begins in your mind. It begins with a simple thought like, "I am going to laugh more in life." If you allow yourself to laugh, heartily and cathartically, then you are going to reap all the benefits of laughter. You have to challenge yourself each day to find opportunities to laugh.

If stress is a thought acted upon, then so, too, is laughter, manifested in a *"ha, ha"* and a *"ho, ho!"* It is not always easy to laugh; however, you can make the best of every "now" moment you have. Yesterday is dead and gone. You don't know what tomorrow holds. Don't waste your life thinking about

Born To Cathart

yesterday or tomorrow. Yet what do you do when life hands you a tough situation?

I remember when I was a child and came down with a bad cold. Usually, my Mom would keep me home from school. Also, my Dad would buy me a new coloring book and a big box of Crayolas. To this day, I still love the smell of crayons. If one could get addicted to Crayolas, I'd be hooked. (Maybe that's why I became a teacher–so I could sniff crayons all day.)

When I would open that box of crayons, my eyes feasted on all the delicious looking colors stacked row upon row. The aroma filled my nostrils and mind with rainbow visions. Before long, I'd be coloring those pages with blazing blues, vibrant yellows and crimson reds. At first, I just picked any pretty color and scribbled on the page. I didn't pay very much attention to the lines. However, when I got a little older and more mature, I understood that those lines served a purpose.

It became a challenge for this six year old child to color within the lines. That went on for quite some time until I understood a little bit more about coloring. As I got older, I looked at the pictures I had colored and knew something was still missing. The pictures were pretty, but they lacked depth and definition. So, unknowingly, I turned to my box of forty-eight crayons and noticed, perhaps for the first time, a group of somber looking colors. I hadn't paid much attention to these colors in the past. They didn't leap out of the box and excite me when I was young. Initially, I went for the dazzling colors and shied away from the dark crayons. Now, being older, something within told me I needed to experience the dark crayons.

I took the black crayon in my hand and studied it carefully. Then, I looked down at the coloring book. Without being instructed, I began to outline the pictures I had just colored. Suddenly, the radiant reds became more radiant. The brilliant blues became bluer. The yellows jumped off the page with excitement. The black crayon had added the depth and definition that was missing from my other pictures. It was the black crayon that made my rainbow colors come alive.

It is also this way with your life. There will be events that will come into your life which are like black crayons. Initially, you won't want to play with those colors. You won't even want to pick them up. You will want to stay as far away from that somberness as possible. However, when you get older and understand more, you realize that these events outline, highlight and add greater definition to the rainbow colors of your life.

It has been said that one appreciates the sun because one has known the rain. One appreciates joy because one has known sorrow. One appreciates laughter because one has known tears. In life, there will be events where God asks you to turn your attention back to the box of life's crayons and tells you, "Pick up the black crayon. Take this event, stress, sadness, disappointment, despair and outline it!" Fortunately, God does not ask you to color the whole page of your life black. In His wisdom, He lets you know that it is through these events that you can make the living, loving and the laughter more precious and meaningful to you.

❈ ❈ ❈ ❈ ❈ ❈

It was at the 1997 Living Fully with Cancer Conference sponsored by M.D. Anderson Cancer Hospital here in Houston, Texas, that I first used this analogy of black crayons in the closing of my presentation. After the presentation, a woman came up to talk with me. She held a thin, white book in her hand and said, "This is for you." The name of the book was *Fine Black Lines-Reflections on Facing Cancer, Fear and Loneliness,* by Lois Tschetter Hjelmstad. The book focused on the past four years of her life. It contained excerpts from her journal, selected poems and reflections she wrote during her journey of having breast cancer. I want you to read the notation that was written by the author on May 16, 1993.

"Today was truly special. The church looked lovely for my students' big spring recital. The two pianos gleaming on the

Born To Cathart

stage. *The black ink notes dancing on manuscript paper on the walls and the sanctuary overflowing with baskets of red geraniums.*

There were many more guests than I would have expected. The students played well and the joyful Spirit that filled the room was almost palpable. At the end of the program, I stood on my head. For the past 30 years I did this on the last day of class for each group of students. The children always loved it, but this year since I am not going to offer the bonus week of lessons after the recital, I decided to add another light touch to the program. I wasn't sure my arms would be strong enough to support my body today. Although I have stood on my head many times since the mastectomies, my practice headstands two days ago were unsuccessful. But I decided to try anyway, and just to laugh if I failed. The important thing is to try. Four years ago, I wouldn't have considered taking such a risk, but nothing seems much like a risk anymore and my sense of decorum has yielded to my desire to find joy in everything I do. I hadn't planned to make any closing remarks, but when I was preparing for the recital this morning, the following thoughts came to me and I decided to share them.

> It is to this time that I have come—
> to an afternoon such as this—
> full of music, children, laughter,
> learning, joy
> It is to this time that I have come—
> to claim my small space on the planet
> to share what I can do
> to stretch my talent
> to take a risk
> It is to this time that I have come—
> but I couldn't be here without each of you
> sharing, laughing, loving, encouraging.
> Thank you so much.

Born To Cathart

As we had refreshments, the children and their parents were beaming. Again and again, the children came up and hugged me to say goodbye for the summer. As we embraced, I realized once more how much joy I find in teaching."

The author said, "*I have come to a time such as this. But I couldn't be here without each of you sharing, laughing, loving, encouraging."* The journey of life from then to now is filled with laughter. It is filled with joy. That's what makes the journey worth the trip.
Thanks, Lois. I couldn't have said it any better.

❋ ❋ ❋ ❋ ❋ ❋ ❋

I may not be the world's funniest comedienne. In fact, I preface all my presentations by stating that I am not a stand-up comic. However, I am a teacher. It is my hope and prayer that I can teach you that . . . ***YOU WERE BORN TO CATHART!***

Born To Cathart

Born To Cathart

*It is requisite for the relaxation of the mind
that we make use, from time to time,
of playful deeds and jokes...*
          Thomas Aquinas

Chapter Nine

Pull My Finger!

I know that in a few moments, you are going to finish reading this book and, perhaps, close it forever. So I want to give you a gift that you can take with you to remind you to *cathart!*

Actually, it is a little technique you can use to remind yourself to take a healing interval of laughter for fifteen seconds. It is your index finger. My father taught this to me when I was a little girl. In fact, it was the only lesson in life I learned immediately. I didn't need a repeat lesson. Apparently, it was a tradition handed down to all the men in our family.

Whenever my father suffered from "intestinal distress", he would ask me to help him out. He would catch me in an unsuspecting moment and say, "Marion, come here and *pull my finger!*" My father, who was a policeman all his life, but when you pulled his finger he became an exterminator and flooded the air with his aromatic odors. (He always tried to blame it on the dog!)

Well, I want to give you a new definition of *"Pull My Finger.* From now on, when you see someone who is down, depressed, discouraged, overwhelmed, stressed out and needs a laugh break, you can look them straight in the eye and say, *"Pull My Finger!"* That little expression will be a signal for all to laugh heartily for fifteen "cathartic" seconds. You may want to get a group of stressed-out friends together and have a "communal-catharting" party.

Born To Cathart

One word of caution! Make sure the individuals you are trying to help understand the new definition of *"Pull My Finger"*. Otherwise, you may get a response you don't appreciate.

So, one more time, I want to lead you in that cheer, *I WAS BORN TO CATHART!* Only this time, when you get to the word *cathart*, I want you to stand to your feet, raise your *cathartic finger* in the air, bring it down with a resounding "YES"! And, if someone's there with you, have them pull your finger and laugh heartily for fifteen seconds. Are you ready? Nice and loud and with true conviction in your heart say . . .

   I . . .
      WAS . . .
         BORN . . .
            TO . . .
               CATHART!
               PULL MY FINGER!

God bless, Marion

Born To Cathart

BIBLIOGRAPHY

Cameron, Julia. The Artists' Way. New York. G.P. Putnam's & Sons, 1992.

Cousins, Norman. Anatomy of an Illness. New York: Bantam Books, 1981.

———. Head First: The Biology of Hope and the Healing Power of the Human Spirit. New York: Penguin Books, 1989.

———. The Healing Heart: Antidotes to Panic and Helplessness. New York: W.W. Norton & Company, 1983.

Gray, John, Ph.D. Men Are From Mars; Women Are From Venus. New York: Harper Collins, 1992.

Hjelmstad, Lois Tschetter. Fine Black Lines: Reflections on Facing Cancer, Fear and Loneliness. Colorado: Mulberry Hill Press, 1993.

Robinson, Vera M. Humor and the Health Professions: The Therapeutic Use of Humor in Health Care. New Jersey: Slack Inc., 1991.

Samra, Cal, and Rose Samra. Holy Humor. Tennessee: Thomas Nelson Publishers, 1997.

Sapolsky, Robert M. Why Zebras Don't Get Ulcers: A Guide to Stress, Stress-Related Diseases, and Coping. New York: W.H. Freeman and Company, 1994.

Williams, Redford, M.D., and Virginia Williams, Ph.D. Anger Kills. New York: Harper Collins, 1993.

Born To Cathart

(If you would like to talk to Marion, tell her one of your true-life amusing stories, just provide feedback, or place a credit card order for tapes or T-Shirts, you can e-mail her at: MPietz@worldnet.att.net. See below for more details about ordering materials.)

MORE FROM MARION!

"Born To Cathart" T-Shirts

Short Sleeve	(L, XL)	16.00
	XXL	18.00
	XXXL	20.00
Long Sleeve	(L, XL)	20.00
	(XXL	24.00

Humorous Tape Recordings

"Laughing Your Way Through Stress" (Live recording) 10.00
Laugh Track (10 minutes of just laughter) 5.00
The Art of Therapeutic Storytelling (Live Recording) 10.00
"What You Know Can Help You!" Teambuilding
    (Live Recording) 10.00

Music Recordings

"I'll Endure"
    (Christian Songs of Worship & Meditation) 10.00
"Just For Fun"
    (Humorous Songs of Pentecostal Church Life) 10.00
Broken Homes & Bruised Kids
    (Songs About & To Hurting Kids) 10.00

Texas residents add 8.25% sales tax.
Shipping, postage and handling add $1.95.

Need more "Born To Cathart" books, call (281) 360-4729 to order.

Born To Cathart

ORDER FORM (please print)

DATE: ---

NAME ---

ADDRESS --

PHONE : --

Make checks and / or money orders to Humor Therapy.

CREDIT CARD SALES

Card (check): VISA ____ MasterCard ____ Discover ____

American Exp. ____

Number on the card: _____

Exp. Date ---

Name on Account: --

Signature: --

Date: ---

$10.00 fee on all returned checks.

Call (281) 360-4729 to order by phone
or mail order form to:
Humor Therapy
3106 Glade Springs
Kingwood, Texas 77339

Born To Cathart

Born To Cathart

The Real End